NGONI

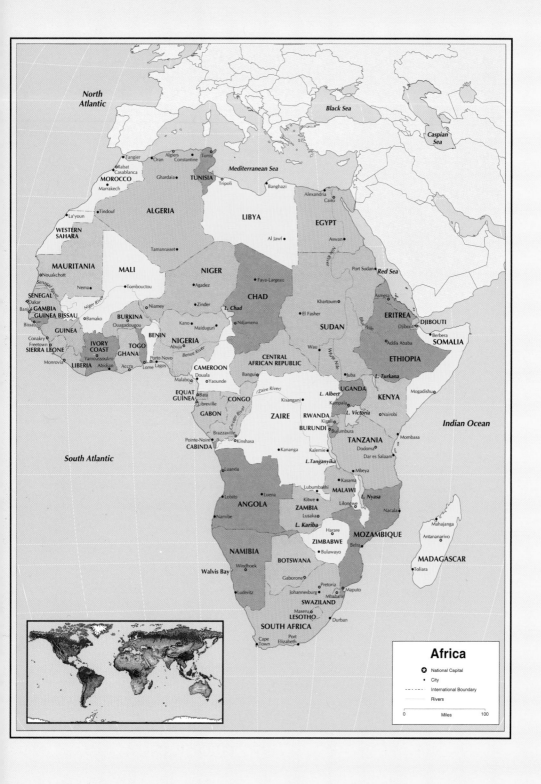

North
Atlantic

Black Sea

Caspian
Sea

Tangier
Rabat
Casablanca
MOROCCO
Marrakech

Algiers
Oran Constantine
Tunis
TUNISIA

Ghardaia

Mediterranean Sea

Tripoli

Banghazi

Alexandria
Cairo

La'youn
Tindouf

WESTERN
SAHARA

ALGERIA

LIBYA

EGYPT

Aswan

MAURITANIA
Nouakchott

Nema

MALI

Tamanrasset

Al Jawf

Port Sudan

Red Sea

SENEGAL
Dakar
Banjul GAMBIA
GUINEA BISSAU
Bissau
GUINEA
Conakry
Freetown
SIERRA LEONE
Monrovia
LIBERIA

Tombouctou

Niger River

Bamako

Niamey

NIGER

Agadez

Zinder

L. Chad

Faya-Largeau

Khartoum

CHAD

El Fasher

SUDAN

Asmera
ERITREA
DJIBOUTI
Djibouti
Berbera
SOMALIA

BURKINA
Ouagadougou

Kano

Maiduguri

Ndjamena

Wau

Blue Nile

Addis Ababa

IVORY
COAST
Yamoussoukro
Abidjan

BENIN
TOGO
GHANA
Accra

NIGERIA
Abuja

Benue River

Porto Novo
Lome Lagos

CAMEROON
Douala

CENTRAL
AFRICAN REPUBLIC

Bangui

White Nile

Juba

L. Turkana

ETHIOPIA

Mogadishu

EQUAT.
GUINEA
Bata
Libreville

Malabo

Yaounde

(Zaire River)

CONGO

Kisangani

L. Albert
Kampala

UGANDA

KENYA
Nairobi

GABON

ZAIRE

RWANDA
Kigali
BURUNDI
Bujumbura

L. Victoria

Mombasa

Indian Ocean

South Atlantic

Brazzaville
Pointe-Noire
Kinshasa
CABINDA

Kananga

Kalemie

TANZANIA
Dodoma
Dar es Salaam

Luanda

L. Tanganyika

Mbeya
Kasama

Lobito
Luena

ANGOLA

Namibe

Lubumbashi
Kitwe
ZAMBIA
Lusaka

MALAWI
Lilongwe

L. Nyasa

Nacala

L. Kariba

Harare

ZIMBABWE
Bulawayo

Beira

MOZAMBIQUE

Mahajanga

Antananarivo

NAMIBIA

Walvis Bay

Windhoek

BOTSWANA

Gaborone

Pretoria

Johannesburg

Maputo
Mbabane
SWAZILAND
Maseru
LESOTHO
Durban

MADAGASCAR

Toliara

Luderitz

SOUTH AFRICA

Cape
Town

Port
Elizabeth

Africa

National Capital
City
International Boundary
Rivers

0   Miles   100

NGONI

Nwankwo T. Nwaezeigwe

THE ROSEN PUBLISHING GROUP, INC.
NEW YORK

Published in 1997 by The Rosen Publishing Group, Inc.
29 East 21st Street, New York, NY 10010

First Edition·

Manufactured in the United States of America

Library of Congress Cataloging-in-Publication Data

Nwaezeigwe, Nwankwo T.
   Ngoni / Nwankwo T. Nwaezeigwe. — 1st ed.
     p. cm. — (The heritage library of African peoples)
   Includes bibliographical references and index.
   Summary: Describes the culture, history, and contemporary life of the Ngoni people of Malawi.
   ISBN 0-8239-2006-2
   1. Ngoni (African people)—Juvenile literature. [1. Ngoni (African people)] I. Title. II. Series.
DT3192.N44N94   1996
968.97′00496391—dc20   96-22945
                                            CIP
                                            AC

Contents

Introduction   6

1. Origins of the Ngoni   9

2. The Ngoni Migrations   18

3. Ngoni Society   29

4. Religion and Customs   42

5. The Coming of *Azungu*

    (the Whites)   55

Glossary   61

For Further Reading   62

Index   63

INTRODUCTION

THERE IS EVERY REASON FOR US TO KNOW something about Africa and to understand its past and the way of life of its peoples. Africa is a rich continent that has for centuries provided the world with art, culture, labor, wealth, and natural resources. It has vast mineral deposits, fossil fuels, and commercial crops.

But perhaps most important is the fact that fossil evidence indicates that human beings originated in Africa. The earliest traces of human beings and their tools are almost two million years old. Their descendants have migrated throughout the world. To be human is to be of African descent.

The experiences of the peoples who stayed in Africa are as rich and as diverse as of those who established themselves elsewhere. This series of books describes their environment, their modes of subsistence, their relationships, and their customs and beliefs. The books present the variety of languages, histories, cultures, and religions that are to be found on the African continent. They demonstrate the historical linkages between African peoples and the way contemporary Africa has been affected by European colonial rule.

Africa is large, complex, and diverse. It encompasses an area of more than 11,700,000 square miles. The United States, Europe, and India could fit easily into it. The sheer size is an indication of the continent's great variety in geography, terrain, climate, flora, fauna, peoples, languages, and cultures.

Much of contemporary Africa has been shaped by European colonial rule, industrialization, urbanization, and the demands of a world economic system. For more than seventy years, large regions of Africa were ruled by Great Britain, France, Belgium, Portugal, and Spain. African peoples from various ethnic, linguistic, and cultural backgrounds were brought together to form colonial states.

For decades Africans struggled to gain their independence. It was not until after World War II that the colonial territories became independent African states. Today, almost all of Africa is ruled by Africans. Large numbers of Africans live in modern cities. Rural Africa is also being transformed, and yet its people still engage in many of their customs and beliefs.

Contemporary circumstances and natural events have not always been kind to ordinary Africans. Today, however, new popular social movements and technological innovations pose great promise for future development.

George C. Bond, Ph.D., Director
Institute of African Studies
Columbia University, New York

The effects of many migrations have caused the different Ngoni groups to develop complex, and often differing, cultures. Seen here is a Ngoni dancer from Malawi.

chapter

1

ORIGINS OF THE NGONI

THE PEOPLE KNOWN TODAY AS THE NGONI live in scattered kingdoms and chiefdoms in eastern Central Africa. There are many differences between these kingdoms. However, they share the fact that they all once lived far to the south. Their ancestors' original home was near the northeast coast of present-day South Africa; they were once part of the Nguni peoples who were settled there. In the early 1800s, wars in southern Africa forced some Nguni groups to leave their homelands. They chose the name "Ngoni" instead of "Nguni." The new name may have been chosen because it was easier to pronounce for the peoples that the Ngoni met in the north.

The Ngoni migrations lasted several decades and covered thousands of miles. From 1818 to 1877, the Ngoni groups were continually at war; they conquered and absorbed many of the other

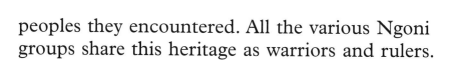

peoples they encountered. All the various Ngoni groups share this heritage as warriors and rulers.

However, each Ngoni kingdom was influenced by the particular mix of enemies it defeated and absorbed. Today few Ngoni speak their original Nguni language; they have adopted the languages of the people they ruled or settled among.

Each Ngoni kingdom had different experiences when Europe attempted to colonize the region. Ultimately, all groups lost their power and authority in what later became the countries of Malawi, Zambia, Mozambique, and Tanzania. When the British, Germans, and Portuguese established boundaries between these countries in 1891, they divided and interfered with several Ngoni chiefdoms. Today these boundaries still create difficulties for the Ngoni chiefdoms, who experience different circumstances in the modern countries where they now live.

Because the Ngoni have merged with neighboring peoples—including the Chewa, Tumbuka, Tonga, Nyanja, and Yao—their population is difficult to estimate. There are about 200,000 Ngoni in Mozambique, 210,000 in Tanzania, 300,000 in Zambia, and 608,000 in Malawi. This book focuses on the largest Ngoni groups in Malawi: the Jere Ngoni of the M'Mbelwa kingdom and the Maseko Ngoni of the Gomani kingdom. Both of these chiefdoms spill over into

Origins of the Ngoni

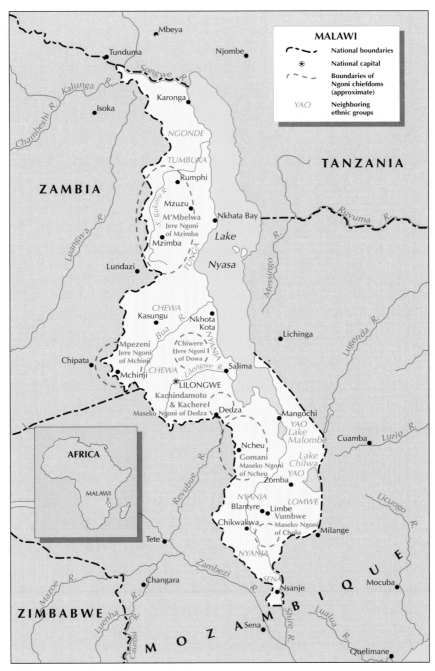

The Ngoni of Malawi consist of two main groups: the Jere and the Maseko, each with smaller divisions. This book focuses on the Maseko of the Gomani kingdom and the Jere of the M'Mbelwa kingdom.

neighboring countries. The region also contains smaller Maseko and Jere Ngoni chiefdoms.

Today the M'Mbelwa Jere and Gomani Maseko kingdoms are ruled by paramount chiefs. They are descendants of the great chiefs who led their people out of South Africa more than 150 years ago.

▼ THE NGUNI ORIGINS OF THE NGONI ▼

In the early 1800s the northeast coast of South Africa was inhabited by a number of small chiefdoms, including the Ndwandwe, Ngwane, Mthethwa, Zulu, and Jere. Together, these peoples are referred to as the North Nguni.

Although the Nguni did some farming and trading, their main occupation was herding cattle. In all Nguni societies, cattle were very important. Cattle provided food and clothing. They were the basis of the economy and all business transactions, so ownership of cattle determined someone's wealth and status in society. Cattle were also important to families. Before a couple could marry, cattle were given to the bride's family to compensate them for losing a member of the family. This was called a bride-price.

Nguni men were closely associated with cattle. As boys they herded cattle and as warriors, raided them. In addition, important men were buried in a hide inside the cattle kraal,

Since cattle were so important to Ngoni society, the cattle kraal, or corral, was central to the Ngoni cultures and villages, and important figures were often buried there. Seen here is a group of Ngoni men in a kraal.

or corral. The Nguni loved their cattle. Every animal in the herd was named and recognized for its individual markings and character.

Cattle were also very important in the Nguni religion, which emphasized contact with ancestors. Nguni believed that important ancestors could only be consulted through a sacrifice of cattle. The meat was regarded as food shared between the living and the dead; in other words, cattle connected the living and the dead. These attitudes toward cattle remain strong among many Nguni peoples today, including the Ngoni.

The early 1800s brought many changes to the Nguni in southern Africa. Population growth and drought brought the various chiefdoms into conflict over scarce grazing land. Also, trade with Europeans on the coast was very profitable, and chiefs competed to control the trade.

Two Nguni kingdoms became particularly powerful—the Ndwandwe led by Zwide, and the

Mthethwa led by Dingiswayo. Each controlled smaller chiefdoms that would support the larger kingdoms during wartime. During this time, Zwide controlled two small chiefdoms that later became Ngoni: the Jere of Chief Zwangendaba, who lived around the Hluhluwe River west of Lake St. Lucia; and the Maseko, who lived in the Pongolo River region, south of present-day Swaziland. Both of these groups regarded Zwide as their great chief, *inkosi*. They fought with him against his rival, Dingiswayo.

One of the areas controlled by Dingiswayo was the small Zulu kingdom. A key figure in the region was Shaka, the illegitimate son of Chief Senzangakona, who ruled the Zulu. Because of his bravery as a warrior, Shaka was noticed by Dingiswayo, and was made a commander in the larger Mthethwa kingdom.

In 1816 Shaka's father, Senzangakona, died. Because Shaka was illegitimate, his claim to the Zulu throne was weak. However, Dingiswayo loaned Shaka some Mthethwa soldiers so he could seize the Zulu kingdom. This began Shaka's career as a warrior-king.

In 1818 Zwide captured Dingiswayo and executed him, thus making himself the most powerful leader in the region. Shaka took control of the great Mthethwa kingdom that had once reigned over the Zulu. Zwide realized that Shaka was becoming a dangerous rival. He

Ngoni rulers are direct descendants of chiefs who once lived in present-day South Africa under the authority of Zwide, king of the Ndwandwe. Seen here are Chief Njolomole (left), Paramount Chief Gomani (right) and his *induna*, Kantula (seated).

decided to attack the Mthethwa again. In the
resulting battle at Gqokoli Hill, Shaka used a
new battle tactic. Although they were out-
numbered, Shaka's forces stayed on Gqokoli Hill
and fought off the Ndwandwe, killing Zwide's
five sons.

Zwide was enraged. Determined to defeat
Shaka, he quickly gathered his largest army ever.
When Shaka discovered the size of Zwide's
army, he decided to try guerrilla hit-and-run
tactics. First he withdrew his people, their cattle,
and all the available food, so that the enemy
would not be able to find supplies. Zwide's army
advanced as far as the Tugela River, hoping to
battle Shaka, but found no sign of the Zulu
army. With nothing to eat, the Ndwandwe army
weakened daily. One night, as the tired
Ndwandwe army lay fast asleep, a small group
of Shaka's soldiers crept into their camp and lay
down among them. Before daybreak, each Zulu
soldier had plunged his spear into a sleeping
enemy and fled, leaving many dead.

This tactic so unnerved Zwide's powerful
army that it retreated. But the Zulu army pur-
sued the Ndwandwe slowly and quietly. When
the Ndwandwe reached the Mhlatuze River that
formed the boundary between the two kingdoms, the Zulu attacked them with all their
force. Thus, in 1818, Zwide and his allies were
defeated and scattered.▲

MUSIC AND DANCE

During their military period, the Ngoni performed a special regimental dance, called Ngoma, which combined singing, leaping, and feet stamping. Its strenuous nature demonstrated the dancers' strength. Later the Ngoma became a general entertainment dance involving men and women, young and old.

Before going to battle, warriors used to perform the Ligubo dance in the kraal for the whole community. On their return from war, they entered the kraal and sang the *imihubo* song to announce their return. This called the community to gather in the kraal to welcome them. During the reception, warriors who had distinguished themselves in battle were honored by dancing the Ligiya, a dance of heroes. Every Ngoni warrior hoped to be called to perform the Ligiya one day.

Citele is a competition dance held after each harvest by teams of young girls from different villages. Unsindo is a special pre-marriage dance performed by individual women to signify that they are ready for marriage.

Today in Malawi the Ngoni tradition of dancing before their leaders is maintained and incorporated into the celebration of Independence Day and other state occasions.

Ngoma, once a regimental military dance, has become a form of entertainment for many Ngoni. Seen here are a group of Ngoni schoolchildren performing the Ngoma dance.

2

THE NGONI MIGRATIONS

IN THE TIME OF GREAT UNREST FOLLOWING Zwide's defeat, many groups attempted to escape Shaka. Zwide's great army scattered in five major sections, each led by a different general. As these groups moved, they both attacked and were attacked by the people they encountered. The turmoil within the northern Nguni chiefdoms had a ripple effect. The entire region was unstable and many communities were uprooted. This period of southern African history is called the Mfecane (pronounced mm-fah-kah-nee), meaning "the great scattering."

Today's scholars find it difficult to determine the specific history of this region during that era. However, we know that fleeing Nguni leaders tried to find secure places to settle, and sometimes they joined forces with each other for short periods. It was at this time that the Jere and Maseko, which both became important

Ngoni groups, began their migrations. For many years they fought various peoples and absorbed captives. Approximately twenty years after their defeat by Shaka, both groups crossed the Zambezi River and headed north.

▼ THE JERE ▼

Historians believe that the Jere, led by Zwangendaba, crossed the Zambezi (Ukwembe) River on November 19, 1835. According to Jere oral history, the crossing occurred during an eclipse, which can be precisely dated. By this time Zwangendaba was a strong and famous leader. He had increased his numbers by absorbing many Tonga, Kalanga, and Rozwi peoples in what later became Zimbabwe.

After crossing the Zambezi, Zwangendaba settled for some time at a place called Mkoko (among the Nsenga people). From there, he raided surrounding peoples. In approximately 1839, the Jere migrated north, passing west of present-day Chipata (Fort Jameson). Entering the region that is now Malawi, the Jere Ngoni settled for four years near the Mawiri Lakes. They defeated the Tumbuka, Chewa, and Nsenga people in the area. Other groups that had strong leaders (including the Bemba, Lunda, and Kamanga) were not defeated.

The Jere then migrated to the territory of the Fipa people, between Lakes Malawi and

In 1842 the Maseko Ngoni crossed the Shire River. They began to raid the Matengo people of Mozambique and other groups. Today the Shire is used primarily for transportation and fishing.

Tanzania. The king of Fipa had learned that the Ngoni planned to raid his country and quickly sent a peaceful message to Zwangendaba. As a result the Ngoni did not destroy the Fipa kingdom when they reached it in approximately 1842. Once there Zwangendaba built a capital named Mapupo, which means "dreams." For the following two years they raided the neighboring people (mainly the Sukuma and Msafwa).

In 1845 Zwangendaba died in Mapupo and was buried in an ox hide at Chapota, close to the Nyinaluzi River. He was a ruler who had fled war only to spend his life going from battle to battle. He was a great warrior and organizer who, in some respects, revolutionized central Africa. Because of his outstanding achievements as a nation builder, Zwangendaba is regarded as the father of the Ngoni. However, he was not the only Ngoni leader.

▼ THE MASEKO ▼

The Maseko Ngoni crossed the Zambezi around 1839, led by Mputa. They settled near Domwe Mountain in Malawi, absorbing many Ntumba people who also herded cattle.

In 1842 the Maseko crossed the Shire River and headed up the opposite side of Lake Malawi from the Jere. They raided the Matengo in Mozambique. They also conquered the Ndendeuli and Pangwa near Songea in present-day Tanzania. There Mputa established a capital called Ngongoma. The Maseko Ngoni were happily settled here until events in the Jere Ngoni kingdom began to affect them.

▼ TROUBLE IN THE JERE KINGDOM ▼

Following Zwangendaba's death in 1845, a dispute broke out among the Jere Ngoni about who should become their new leader. This situation sheds some light on various Ngoni customs.

Zwangendaba's two sons, Mbelwa (also called Mombera) and Mpezeni, were too young to reign when their father died. Zwangendaba's younger brother Ntabeni took over as regent until one of the princes was ready to rule. The choice between the two princes was a difficult and complicated one that involved Ngoni

In the 1800s an Ngoni king could have more than one wife, though he had to choose one to bear his heir. The one he chose was called the Great Wife. Seen here is G. L. Jere with his Great Wife and family.

customs and beliefs. The question of who was the rightful heir divided the Jere people.

According to Nguni custom, men could have more than one wife. The wife chosen by the king to bear his heir was called the Great Wife. Zwangendaba's Great Wife was Zwide's niece, who died childless. A Great Wife who was childless could, however, bring another woman into the Great House to bear children for the king. This practice was called *nshlanze*. The children born under the *nshlanze* custom were considered to be the children of the Great Wife. Thus the first son of the *nshlanze* could become the rightful heir to the throne.

Mpezeni was Zwangendaba's eldest son, born with the *nshlanze* Sosera Nqumayo. By custom he was heir to the Ngoni throne. However, an event occurred during Mpezeni's childhood that altered his unquestionable right to succeed his father.

When Mpezeni was still a baby, one of the women in the Great House served Zwangendaba some beer. Zwangendaba saw some hairs floating in the beer. This offense violated the Ngoni's strict rules of cleanliness and led to a suspicion that the hairs were placed there for witchcraft. Suspecting that someone in the Great House was trying to kill him, Zwangendaba ordered the Great House to be destroyed. Many of its members were executed. Mpezeni and his mother were hidden from Zwangendaba's wrath by some kind people and escaped death. They were later presented to the king when his anger had cooled; he eventually forgave and accepted them. However, the king had

The descendants of former Ngoni ruler Mbelwa are called the M'Mbelwa Jere Ngoni. Seen here is the present-day Paramount Chief of the M'Mbelwa Ngoni dancing.

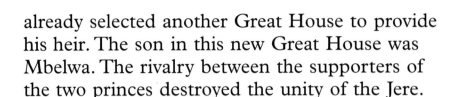

already selected another Great House to provide his heir. The son in this new Great House was Mbelwa. The rivalry between the supporters of the two princes destroyed the unity of the Jere.

▼ SPLITS AMONG THE JERE ▼

When Zwangendaba died, his relative, the regent Ntabeni, supported Mpezeni. Others under Zwangendaba's cousin, Mgayi, supported Mbelwa. Not long after Ntabeni became regent, he died and was replaced by Mgayi. Ntabeni's supporters feared Mgayi and decided to leave. This group later became known as the Tuta Ngoni.

Shortly after this, another group also left the fold, led by Zulu-Gama. They moved to the Songea district, where they met up with the Maseko. They assassinated the Maseko's king, Mputa, in 1847 and drove the Maseko into Mozambique, where the Maseko searched for a place to settle for more than twenty years.

Meanwhile Mgayi led the main Jere group south, to settle between Lakes Malawi and Tanzania, in present-day Malawi. Here Mgayi installed Mbelwa as the new ruler.

When one of Mbelwa's expeditions met with problems, Mpezeni's supporters saw this as a bad omen—a sign that Mbelwa was not the rightful leader. They, too, left the main group. They migrated southwest toward Lake

Malawi has rich natural resources and is ideal for farming. Seen here is Mt. Mulanji in southern Malawi's tea-growing area (top), and a view of Monkey Bay in the south of Lake Malawi.

Bangweolo where they met strong resistance from the Bemba people. They were forced to turn southeast and invade the Nsenga people, who had been devastated by Zwangendaba in 1835. Many Nsenga were captured and combined with earlier Nsenga captives. They constituted the majority of Mpezeni's followers. They finally settled in the present-day Chipata district in Zambia around 1870.

Meanwhile Mbelwa attacked and defeated the Tumbuka kingdom in approximately 1855 and killed their king. The M'Mbelwa Jere settled there in what is now their present territory. Their people were a mixed group, including Swazi, Neungwa, Sotho, Snenga, Sukuma, Nyika, Nkonde, Nkamange, and Chewa. The M'Mbelwa Jere continued to raid the surrounding area and took captives from the Tonga, Henga, Kezembe, and even the Bemba.

The M'Mbelwa sent an expedition southwest of Lake Malawi under the leadership of a Nsenga captive named Chiwere Ndhlovu, who had become a war captain. When the expedition reached the present-day Dowa district of Malawi, the group found good grazing land for their cattle and settled there. They founded an independent Ngoni kingdom among the Chewa.

▼ THE MASEKO ▼
In approximately 1870 the wandering

Maseko Ngoni crossed the Shire River from Mozambique, where they had fled to escape the Jere. In order to resettle in the Domwe areas, where they had lived almost thirty years earlier, the Maseko had to once again defeat the Chewa and Ntumba people who lived there. The Maseko soon split into two groups: one under Gomani, and the other becoming the Kachindamoto and Kachere Maseko. These are the main Maseko of Malawi. The Vumbwe Maseko of southern Malawi are mostly Maseko who were settled there by the British to work the tea plantations.▲

Many aspects of the Nguni government are evident in the modern Ngoni system. Seen here is Chief Mpezeni (seated), holding his royal horse-tail fly whip.

chapter

3

NGONI SOCIETY

THE NGONI GROUPS SHARED A COMMON
Nguni background, which played a major role
in their ability to conquer and control other
groups. In their migrations, they used military
skills learned from the Nguni wars. They also
maintained a strong social structure and strict
rules of behavior. While each group continued to
observe important Nguni customs and traditions, the chiefdoms adopted new practices
along the way. These practices often varied
between Ngoni chiefdoms and kingdoms and
helped define the groups.

▼ NGONI GOVERNMENT ▼

There is evidence that Ngoni government was
similar to the old Nguni system. Under the
Nguni system, the *inkosi* (king or paramount
chief) was the political, military, judicial, religious, and economic leader. He was greeted with

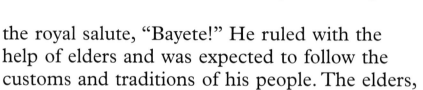

the royal salute, "Bayete!" He ruled with the help of elders and was expected to follow the customs and traditions of his people. The elders, known as *izinduna* (singular: *induna*), included selected village headmen, territorial chiefs, members of the royal family, and some royal officials.

The *izinduna* were the kingdom's most active and important administrators for everyday matters. Every royal official, from the ordinary messenger in the *inkosi*'s palace to the chief military commander, was called *induna*. However, there was always a chief *induna* who supervised the others. He was responsible for advising the *inkosi* on policy and for implementing his policies.

The chief *induna* was often appointed from among the common people. This occurred because members of the royal family, if appointed to such an important position, might revolt against the *inkosi*. Every *inkosi* of the pre-Mfecane (migration) period, from Dingiswayo and Zwide to minor chiefs like Zwangendaba, had a similar pattern of government.

When the Ngoni fled their homelands, the old system was adapted to reflect their new situation. The Ngoni chiefs were able to maintain unity and control over their increasing number of non-Nguni followers. It is estimated that about 1,000 Ngoni crossed the Zambezi; by 1921 the Maseko and Jere Ngoni in Malawi alone had grown to about 250,000. Two tradi-

Several Ngoni homesteads make up a hamlet. Here a group of women from an Ngoni hamlet approach Mawiri Pool to fish.

tional methods of organization helped integrate other groups: the *mafuko* (clan system) and the age-set system.

▼ MAFUKO, THE CLAN SYSTEM ▼

The basic unit of the Ngoni political organization was the household. A number of these households made up a hamlet. In turn, these hamlets formed a village, or *munzi*, while a collection of villages made up the *pfuko* (clan). Finally, the kingdom was divided into territorial units.

Throughout the period of the Ngoni migrations, this structure was strictly observed and maintained. Whenever a migration halted, every household constructed its homes within the area assigned to its *pfuko*, *munzi*, and hamlet. Every new settlement was arranged and regulated according to seniority. Royal villages were specially mapped out and were considered the most senior.

When the Ngoni migration began, members

of the original group attached themselves to one of the leaders of the Jere or Maseko clans. All captives were brought to the *inkosi*, who distributed them among his officials and warriors. Since these men were attached to particular households, hamlets, villages, and clans, the captives became members of their particular masters' households and assumed positions within the social structure. Male captives were also brought into the Ngoni military for their age groups.

▼ THE AGE-SET SYSTEM ▼

Ngoni males were divided into three main sets—herd boys, warriors, and elders. Each had specific tasks and responsibilities.

The Ngoni had no elaborate public celebrations associated with male or female initiation (the rite of passage from adolescence into adulthood). Ngoni children were separated by gender at an early age. As soon as an Ngoni boy got his second teeth, he stopped sleeping in the same room as his *gogo* (grandmother, who also served as a nurse) and joined other boys in a *laweni* or *mphala*—a boys' dormitory. There he learned to herd cattle and make crafts. He also underwent tests of toughness, endurance, and discipline, which prepared him to become a warrior.

In the *laweni*, boys were not allowed to drink milk. Milk was reserved exclusively for small

Ngoni boys, like other young Malawians, learn a variety of skills and crafts. Seen here are a group of boys boating on Lake Chilwa.

children and women. Boys ate with the adult men, who gave them what the men could not finish. The men told the Ngoni boys stories of war and heroism. Failure in war was regarded as the result of moral failings in the individual or group. These tales inspired boys to become warriors and understand the need for the strict discipline of the *laweni*.

When a boy became strong enough to endure long treks, he could be chosen to go to war with a relative as his *udibi* (carrier). As an *udibi*, he looked after the warrior's war kit and food. Through this new assignment, he saw war first-hand and learned what qualities were needed in a successful warrior.

When a *laweni* boy reached puberty, he had to take daily baths in the river before daybreak.

This cold-water routine, called *ukuchayiwa nga'* *manzi* (to be beaten with water), was supposed to build strength and virility. The boy was instructed to obey his seniors and avoid women.

The boy's father invited a doctor to prepare an extremely bitter medicine called *uludengele*. This was regarded as an effective antidote to all weak and sickly symptoms of the Ngoni boy. The drinking of *uludengele* was witnessed by the boy's father and other male relatives. This occasion was known as *ukuunsa*.

The process of becoming a Ngoni man was geared toward becoming a strong, brave, and responsible warrior. In later life men became respected elders who helped make decisions for their society.

▼ GIRLHOOD ▼

Ngoni girls remained under the supervision of the *gogo* until they were married. An upper-class girl also had an *isidandani*—a personal attendant near her own age. The attendant shared in all of the girl's activities up to the time of her marriage. The *gogo* supervised her growth and behavior.

Between the ages of ten and twelve, girls slept together in a dormitory supervised by an older woman. Together, these girls and their attendants bathed, fetched water, and combed their hair. Young women also formed age groups with

Ngoni girls learn a number of domestic and other specialized skills under the supervision of the *gogo*. Above, Ngoni girls pound maize for cooking. Below, Misindo (wedding) dancers display an elaborate beaded hairstyle.

The Nguni military employed tactics of order and complicated formations that they learned in their confrontations with the Zulu. Seen here is a group of Young Pioneers, an Ngoni scout group, marching in file.

other young women, with whom they shared everything until each was married, one after another.

Back at their various homes, girls learned domestic tasks and highly specialized skills. These included brewing beer and making pottery, beadwork, and complicated hairstyles such as the elaborate *ihlutu* style.

At puberty, emphasis was placed on modesty and respect of elders. For example, one knelt when speaking to an elder. Like the boys, girls were taught obedience and endurance as primary virtues. Girls looked to the *gogo* as a role model. They were inspired to become like the *gogo*—to have the same authority and perform the same important roles.

▼ THE NGONI MILITARY ▼
Before Shaka, Nguni warfare was somewhat

theatrical. Enemies faced each other far apart, impressed and intimidated each other with the dances and displays of elaborately dressed warriors, and hurled spears at each other. Shaka was a brilliant military innovator. He introduced a broad-bladed, short stabbing spear called an *assegai* and tough ox-hide shields. When his enemies had cast their spears and were virtually defenseless, Shaka's soldiers rushed in and attacked, using their shields to protect them. Ngoni warriors employed the same weapons on their migrations, contributing to their victories.

Shaka also taught his troops, or *impis*, to attack in "horn formation," a military maneuver in which an army lines up in the shape of a bull's horns. The main unit faced the enemy, while the two "horns" closed on the enemy from the sides. Apart from this, the *impis* were rigidly disciplined and beautifully dressed. Each regiment wore its own uniform and carried shields with matching colors and patterns. The noise they made with war cries and drumming on their shields was impressive and intimidating. The mere sight and sound of these warriors was enough to scare off many enemies. Ngoni warriors later used this approach, combined with the horn formation, to overwhelm their enemies.

Shaka revolutionized Nguni traditions to create a military society. In the past, boys had been initiated into manhood by circumcision. After

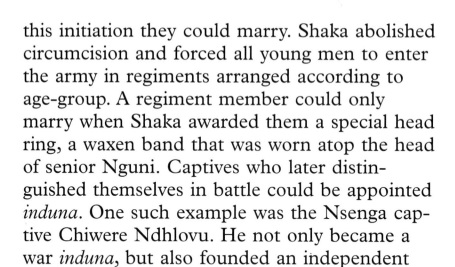

this initiation they could marry. Shaka abolished circumcision and forced all young men to enter the army in regiments arranged according to age-group. A regiment member could only marry when Shaka awarded them a special head ring, a waxen band that was worn atop the head of senior Nguni. Captives who later distinguished themselves in battle could be appointed *induna*. One such example was the Nsenga captive Chiwere Ndhlovu. He not only became a war *induna*, but also founded an independent Ngoni kingdom.

Female captives were married into Ngoni clans. As a result most original Ngoni families were soon mixed with other tribes. These new wives had to follow every detail of Ngoni etiquette, learn how to run a proper Ngoni home, and educate their children in Ngoni customs.

All captives had to pierce their ears like other Ngoni and adopt Ngoni dress. Newcomers were at the lowest rung of the class system, below earlier captives. The original Nguni-speaking leaders, who became known as the Zansi, maintained control and upheld the old Nguni way of life. The Zansi aristocracy furthered its status by adopting behaviors used in the royal court of a great *inkosi*, like Shaka and Zwide.

All these factors aided the integration of numerous captives into Ngoni society. Only a small portion of those who call themselves

Ngoni today are directly descended from the original Jere, Maseko, and other Nguni groups. Most are descendants of captives that were absorbed into the Ngoni communities.

▼ NGONI CAPTIVES ▼

People taken as captives by the Ngoni were often mistreated and mocked by their conquerors on the return from battle. However, once the captives were distributed among the different Ngoni lineages, they became part of the Ngoni society. Captives who had distinguished themselves in battle could also become part of the Ngoni army. This created a large and highly motivated army.

Under Shaka, Nguni society was hierarchical—classified by levels. Shaka, at the top of the hierarchy, was in supreme control of the state and all religious activities. Ngoni society was not as militaristic as that of the Zulu. Warriors could marry before retirement, and the head ring was more a sign of bravery and achievement than a wedding license.

While the Jere and Maseko Ngoni used cultural and military aspects of their Nguni heritage to unify their societies, they also developed and maintained many differences. This could be seen by comparing their warriors, who could be instantly distinguished by the many differences in their dress. Maseko Ngoni warriors wore a wide kidney belt called *chihata*. This was often decorated with beautiful beadwork designs made by their Yao and Chewa wives. They also wore many other beadwork items and decorated their weapons with beads, while the Jere Ngoni did not. The Maseko wore skirts of animal skin that were composed of several ornamental strands; the Jere's were plain. While both Ngoni groups carried clubs, Jere clubs were influenced by their neighbors' taste for figurative designs. They were often carved with human features. Similarly, warriors from other Ngoni groups, like the Mpezeni, could also be easily distinguished by their dress.▲

NGONI SETTLEMENTS

The traditional Ngoni village followed a general Nguni pattern. Before colonization, Ngoni settlements consisted of houses built around a large open space in the center of the village for the cattle kraal, or *chiwaya*. The kraal was built in a horseshoe shape; a gate at the open end served as the major entrance to the village. Next to the gate was the *sangweni*, where men gathered and guarded the cattle.

Outside the kraal, at the end opposite the gate, was the *indlunkulu*. This was the most important dwelling and was occupied by the leader of the kraal. He could be an ordinary village headman, a member of the royal lineage, or an *induna*.

Houses built on each side of the *indlunkulu* belonged to the wives and relatives of the owner of the *indlunkulu*. Behind the *indlunkulu* were a group of huts called the *cigodlo*, which belonged to the married sons and brothers of the owner of the village. Further away were the huts of the *izinduna* (singular *induna*; elder). In larger villages the *izinduna* could establish their own individual kraal and reproduce a similar but smaller village plan with a circle of dwellings.

The sides of the kraal, known as the "horns" of the village, contained the homes of the lesser households. The higher a family's status, the closer their dwellings were to the *indlunkulu*.

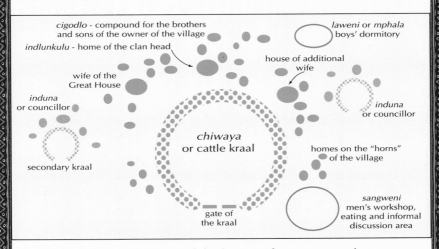

Seen here is a diagram of the layout of an Ngoni settlement.

chapter

4

RELIGION AND CUSTOMS

RELIGION PLAYS AN IMPORTANT ROLE IN most aspects of Ngoni life, including politics, economics, and social affairs.

The Ngoni believe in a supreme God whom they refer to as Umkulumqango, which means the Great Spirit. Umkulumqango is believed to be the Creator and the main source of power, health, rain, victory, and protection from plague.

Next in importance are the spirits of the dead kings, or *amadlozi*. The Ngoni believe that the *amadlozi* stand between Umkulumqango and the people. Next in rank are the *amadlozi* associated with the clans, followed by the family ancestors.

Umkulumqango is generally seen as too remote to listen to humans directly, so people rely on their *amadlozi* as go-betweens. The older the *amadlozi* are, the closer they are to Umkulumqango and the more influential and powerful they are.

The Ngoni have no formal worship of either the Umkulumqango or *amadlozi*. They are only consulted in times of misfortune. The *amadlozi* of the dead kings are the nation's guardians and its major link to Umkulumqango. In times of national crisis—such as drought, epidemic, and war—Umkulumqango is consulted through the kings' ancestral spirits. However, when an important member of a family or clan is sick, or when there are problems with their cattle, Umkulumqango is consulted through the related family or clan *amadlozi*.

When a situation calls for an appeal to Umkulumqango, the Ngoni first consult a diviner, or *isanusi*. A diviner is someone who connects the living with the spirit world by interpreting omens. The diviner determines which of the *amadlozi* must be contacted. One of the cattle must give a sign, usually by urinating, that the *amadlozi* have agreed to receive the prayers. Then the animal is sacrificed in honor of the ancestors, appeals are made to the *amadlozi*, and the meat is "shared" with the ancestors.

Beer and snuff also had religious significance in the past. Many strict rules applied to the preparation, presentation, and consumption of these items. Any neglect or clumsiness in these matters offended the ancestors and insulted others. All the items associated with these three "foods" of the ancestors were sacred and

Ngoni men are excellent carvers, as demonstrated by their elaborate meat plates, milk pails, dance staffs, and other items. Here an Ngoni man prepares a leather shield.

carefully guarded. These items included wooden meat platters and containers, beer pots, and snuff holders. Meat plates were intricately carved by men, blackened, and kept in the sacred area of the house or close to the kraal. Women used a special process to produce strong black beer pots, and these were revered. For both items, their color associated them with the ancestors. Women spent six days making traditional beer, a nourishing drink with very little alcohol. Beer drinking usually took place next to the kraal. The ancestors are always considered to be present whenever people drink beer, even today.

Snuff was a symbolic material, closely associated with Ngoni clans, who each had their own recipes for making it. Men and women had their own snuff containers. These were intensely

Since beer and snuff had religious significance in Ngoni societies, their preparation was careful and time-consuming. Seen here is an Ngoni woman brewing beer, a nourishing drink with little alcohol in it.

personal items that nobody else was allowed to touch. Sharing snuff with someone was an intimate display of trust. Great care was involved in making a snuff container. A scooped-out fruit or small gourd was smoked until it had a rich patina (surface appearance); then it was soaked in cream to seal and polish it. The sweet smell reminded the user of milk and cattle, and thus wealth. Sometimes honey was poured into the container to flavor the snuff.

▼ BURIAL ▼

In most traditional African belief systems, death is not the end of existence. Death turns a person into a spirit. In the spirit world, a dead relative who led a good life on earth is expected

Ngoni kept snuff in special containers, which were intensely personal items that no one else was allowed to touch. Seen here is an Ngoma dancer with his snuff container.

to see to the well-being of his or her living relatives, acting as a messenger between the living and Umkulumqango. On the other hand, people who led bad lives become evil spirits, causing havoc for their relations instead of helping them.

There is a strong belief among the Ngoni that the relative must be buried correctly in order to enter and settle in the spirit world.

In the past all Ngoni were wrapped in an ox hide and buried in a sitting position. The body was seated on a shelf in a circular grave and made to face southeast, toward the ancestral home of the Ngoni.

The head of a household was buried inside the cattle kraal, at the sacred side opposite the entrance. The senior wife was buried nearby, but

46

The Ngoni take great care in the burial of a relative so that he or she will be a benevolent spirit. Seen here is an M'Mbelwa Jere king's grave, properly located within the kraal in a circular shape.

on the opposite side of the kraal fence. Similarly, others were buried at different distances from the head of the household, depending on their rank. After the burial, the kraal was no longer used, and dense vegetation was allowed to grow in it. Even today, nobody visits such sacred burial places without permission from the clan head of the area.

Personal objects, especially ones associated with the ancestors, were buried with the deceased. This explains why few old meat and snuff containers, weapons, tools, clothes, and similar objects survive today. People had to make copies of objects they wanted to keep. After death, personal items were usually broken at the *sangweni*, the place near the entrance to the kraal where mature men would gather, talk, and make items of leather and basketry.

The family could decide to save some objects in order to remember the deceased and promote communication with the ancestors. The spear of an important man is always kept, even today, because it is his heir's sign of legitimacy. At a special ceremonial "washing of the spear," clan relatives witness the spear being "washed" with earth, in which all ancestors are buried. The spear is then plunged into the heart of a bull, reinforcing the link between cattle and the ancestors. After this, the heir officially takes control of the family. Maseko and Jere Ngoni approached the funerals of their paramount chiefs differently. The Maseko *inkosi* was cremated with his objects and an attendant known as the "royal shadow." Today Christianity has affected burials. Graves may now

The spear of an important Ngoni man is always given to his heir as a sign of his legitimacy. Seen here is an Ngoni man with his ancestral spear.

be set apart from the kraal and marked with walls—as in the case of the Jere paramounts M'Mbelwa II and III. In the Mpezeni kingdom today, people are buried in coffins, but an animal skin is placed on top of the casket—a clear combination of old and new customs. Many Ngoni have stopped burying more traditional items, especially in the case of important people, such as the *inkosi*. Although M'Mbelwa II was buried in 1891 with ivory tusks, lion and leopard skins, and personal objects, when M'Mbelwa III died in 1993, the Jere ordered all historical items to be left out of the grave.

▼ MARRIAGE AND DIVORCE ▼

Marriage among the Ngoni was and still is greatly cherished. The Ngoni had a very strict moral code, especially regarding premarital sex. A girl who lost her virginity before marriage was less desirable as a wife. Her parents would receive fewer cattle upon her marriage, and this disgraced her family and age-mates. She would also be disqualified from participating in the *umsindo* celebration, which was a kind of puberty ceremony showing that she was ready for marriage. Boys and young men were also strongly discouraged from premarital sex and early marriage.

Men between the ages of twenty-five and thirty were the nucleus of the Ngoni fighting

force and were not allowed to marry for two major reasons. First, early marriage was believed to weaken the warrior's effectiveness and bravery. Second, it was believed that if a man went to war after sleeping with a woman, he not only risked being killed in the battle, but could cause the defeat of the entire army. Because of these factors, Ngoni society frowned on matters of immorality, and imposed strict rules about marriage among the people.

Among many Ngoni groups, marriage customs closely followed the Nguni pattern. Marriage consisted of four stages. The first included choosing a partner and getting the consent of the two families involved. This was followed by negotiating the number of cattle to be paid as *lobola* (bride-price) to the bride's family. The third stage involved a series of feasts, which gave form and character to the marriage ceremony. The last ceremony was the acceptance of the new wife into her new home in the groom's household.

There were many ways in which the Ngoni could select their marriage partners. A young man could, on seeing a young woman, indicate to her family his interest in marrying her. On the other hand, marriages could be arranged by parents without the consent of the young people. This was common among the ruling aristocracy. However, the most popular method was direct courtship, encouraged by many social activities that brought the sexes together, particularly dancing competitions between different villages. One such dance, the *ingoma*, took place after the harvest.

Once the two families gave their consent, the bulk of the marriage ceremony became the concern of the elders and senior women of the two families. Five feasts were usually held before a young woman was finally regarded as married. The first was the betrothal feast, called Ku-onga, held in the young woman's village. The prospective husband supplied an animal for the feast that signified the formal consent of the young woman's family to the man's proposal.

The next feast, called Ku-tendara, took place in the man's village. Here the bride, accompanied by elder female relatives, visited the man. The man presented beads to his bride and sent a cloth (*mcheka*) to the young woman to give to her mother.

The third feast involved a ceremony in which the woman was allowed to cook in her new husband's house for the first time. The food used in this ceremony was collected from the young woman's village.

The two final feasts were known as the Umnoango and Izinyongo. Umnoango involved beer drinking, while Izinyongo consisted of beer and food. Both items were prepared in the bride's village, but were consumed by both families in the husband's village. These two feasts were the first official meetings between both sets of parents. Once these two feasts concluded, the bride-price was paid, and the woman moved in with her husband. This concluded the marriage ceremony.

Among the Ngoni, divorce was highly discouraged. The only reason a man could divorce his wife was on account of adultery. The woman was not given the same right to divorce her husband. If a woman was divorced before she had children, her parents could be forced to repay the bride-price. However, a man was not allowed to divorce his wife simply because she was childless. In this case, the wife's family could provide the man with one of the wife's sisters as a second wife instead of repaying the *lobola*. This was called *nshlanze*.

However, there are considerable differences in these customs between the various Ngoni groups today. One example of this is the Jere customs. Today, in the Jere area, hoe blades or other valuables replace cattle. Marriage negotiations conclude when the senior wife of the bride's household presents a gift of snuff to the head of the groom's family. Traditionally the snuff is placed in a container and wrapped inside the pelt of a genet cat, a symbol of virility. The package is placed with some beads inside a

The extended courtship period of the Jere Ngoni concludes when the senior wife of the bride's household presents the groom's family with a gift of snuff wrapped in the pelt of a genet cat. Seen here is such a snuff container resting on its pelt.

special bead-covered basket, which is then wrapped in cloth. This exchange of snuff signifies that a close relationship has been formed between the two families and between bride and groom.

▼ INHERITANCE ▼

As noted earlier, the Ngoni settled among the Chewa, Yao, Tumbuka, and Nsenga. These peoples inherit property through their mother's family line under the system of matrilineal descent. However, the Ngoni follow a patrilineal descent system, which means that a man's property is inherited by his eldest son.

Two types of inheritance exist in Ngoni society—land and personal property. Land is

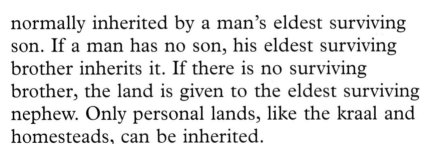

normally inherited by a man's eldest surviving son. If a man has no son, his eldest surviving brother inherits it. If there is no surviving brother, the land is given to the eldest surviving nephew. Only personal lands, like the kraal and homesteads, can be inherited.

All of the land for grazing and farming was owned by the *inkosi*, who held it in trust for his subjects. The *inkosi* gave his subjects the right to use the land and divided it among them. He started by giving land rights to his high-ranking advisers, or *izinduna*. He continued to parcel out the land to the *izinduna* until he reached the level of the village headman. The headmen in turn allotted farming plots to the common people. However, European colonization ended this system, because the colonial governments took control of most of the lands.

A man's personal property, as opposed to his land, is given to his eldest surviving son. If he has no son, the eldest surviving daughter receives the inheritance. If a man dies childless, his father inherits, or, if the father has died, the man's eldest surviving brother or nephew receives the personal property.▲

chapter

5

THE COMING OF *AZUNGU* (THE WHITES)

THE WEAPONS OF THE NGONI THAT HAD brought them many victories against other African groups were no match for European bullets. The colonists wanted Ngoni lands; they clearly recognized the power held by the Ngoni kingdoms and set out to crush them.

The Ngoni kingdoms in Malawi each had a different experience with colonization. Mpezeni's kingdom was split by the colonial boundaries imposed in 1891. This severely reduced the power of the Mpezeni Jere. The M'Mbelwa Jere kingdom in the north of Malawi was far from the colonial centers in southern Malawi and was largely undisturbed. Gomani's Maseko kingdom bore the brunt of repression.

▼ THE GOMANI MASEKO ▼

Colonial authorities imposed a "hut tax" on

the Maseko in 1896, which each house was required to pay. Throughout Africa, colonists used this measure to force Africans to work for them. As a result, most African architecture and settlements changed. Many people abandoned their traditional dwellings, which had separate houses for each wife in favor of bringing families together under one taxable roof.

To protest the forced labor of his subjects, Inkosi Gomani I marched to colonial headquarters on October 6, 1896 and demanded their release. He was turned away by the white colonists. After this insult, Inkosi Gomani I ordered his *impis* to burn down about twenty-seven villages. He was arrested and taken to Blantyre, the colonial capital. On the way, he refused to walk between the horses of his conquerors. Because he refused to cooperate, he was tied to a tree and shot. The British then buried him secretly. This outraged the Maseko, as their own burial traditions consist of an elaborate public cremation.

The Gomani Maseko kingdom was then ruled by regents because Gomani I's rightful heir, Zitongo, was too young to rule. The regents protested that the Gomani kingdom was divided between Malawi (called British Central Africa at that time) and Mozambique (then called Portuguese East Africa). The regents tried to raise an army in Portuguese territory, but they were arrested by the British, along with many headmen and other members of the royal family. Of these only Gomani's brother Zitongo survived. He later crossed into Portuguese territory to rule that portion of the divided kingdom. In 1921 Zitongo was crowned Inkosi Gomani II.

▼ THE MPEZENI JERE ▼

The Mpezeni kingdom was used by colonial companies for mining. Mpezeni allowed mining on his land because of his friendship with a German trader named Carl Weise, who later became a member of the mining company. However, Mpezeni resisted the hut tax.

In January of 1898 Mpezeni awoke one morning to see the *azungu* army camped at the entrance of his kraal. When the Ngoni charged at the white army, they were greeted with machine guns aimed directly at the entrance. Their cowhide shields were useless against the bullets. The once invincible Ngoni warriors fled the battlefield. The invading British force entered the royal village, burned it, and seized half of the cattle. Mpezeni's heir was arrested and shot, together with his wives.

Inkosi Mpezeni, then an old man, was deposed by the British, who appointed his grandson *inkosi*. However, Mpezeni remained the *inkosi* in his people's view. When Mpezeni died six years later, the kingdom was taken over

by Mpezeni's *izinduna* and members of the royal lineage. These regents managed the throne until Mpezeni II came of age.

▼ THE M'MBELWA JERE ▼

M'Mbelwa's kingdom fell under British control peacefully. Several factors accounted for this transition. The first was an incident that demonstrated the benefits of being under "British protection." A British trader named William Ziehl, who pretended to be a government agent, was charged with raiding the Ngoni and stealing ten cattle and ten goats. In 1899 the British colonial court sentenced him to a large fine or six months in prison. This action convinced the Ngoni of M'Mbelwa of British justice.

Second, when M'Mbelwa I died in 1891, the process of choosing a rightful heir weakened the kingdom and its resistance. An unpopular heir was selected to replace M'Mbelwa. This led some of the Jere aristocracy to establish friendly relationships with the British and missionaries without the new *inkosi*'s approval. The missionaries at Livingstonia had a peaceful relationship with the M'Mbelwa people. This was not the case in the other kingdoms where the British agents and missionaries were more commercial.

Also, in 1893, much of the kingdom's herd died of rinderpest, a cattle disease. This negatively affected the social, political, economic, and

Like most other African nations, Malawi fought hard for its independence from European colonial rule. Under the leadership of Hastings Banda, a Chewa, Malawi finally achieved its independence in 1964. Until 1994 Banda ruled Malawi in a dictatorial fashion. Despite the many ethnic groups of Malawi, Banda tried to identify the Malawi nation exclusively with his own Chewa people and culture.

Banda's thirty-year reign ended in 1994. He was pressured into allowing a democratic presidential election, which he lost. His successor was Bakili Muluzi, a former follower of Banda. The new government faces many challenges. Malawi is currently the world's ninth-poorest nation.

As the ninth-poorest nation in the world, Malawi faces many challenges. Seen here is the city of Blantyre, located in southern Malawi.

religious bases of the kingdom, since cattle were such an important part of their lives.

These factors led to a treaty with the British, signed on October 24, 1904, that put the

M'Mbelwa kingdom under effective and total British administration.

British rule of these three Ngoni kingdoms led to a movement away from the old Ngoni traditions. Many of the ethnic groups that had been conquered by the Nguni declared their independence from the Ngoni. Also, the British recognized the independence of these chiefdoms so that the once-powerful Ngoni would not become a threat to them again. The Christian values of the Europeans conflicted with the traditional activities of the Ngoni. For example, the influence of Western civilization was contrary to the traditional discipline under which the Ngoni boys and girls were raised. While there were some positive aspects of the colonial systems, many Ngoni believe that the *azungu* spoiled their land by undermining their society.

▼ CONCLUSION ▼

Today neither the Ngoni, who once conquered other peoples, nor the British, who conquered the Ngoni, are in control. With the departure of the colonists, the Ngoni and their neighbors have been left to forge a new and permanent society where each, regardless of its past, must accommodate the others. This new form of society is the foundation of the modern nation-states of Malawi, Mozambique, Tanzania, and Zambia, where the Ngoni are found today.▲

Glossary

amadlozi Ngoni ancestral spirits.

assegai Broad-bladed, short stabbing spear.

bride-price (lobola) Gifts (usually cattle) given to a woman's family by a male suitor.

gogo Grandmother; nurse for young Ngoni.

hamlet Group of Ngoni households.

hut tax Tax imposed by British colonists, forcing Ngoni to work for wages.

indlunkulu Great house of an Ngoni settlement.

induna Chief commander of the Ngoni military.

inkosi Ngoni chief.

isidandani Personal attendant for upper-class girls.

izinduna Elders; advisors.

kraal Fenced area at the middle of an Ngoni homestead where the cattle are kept and important members of society are buried.

laweni (mphala) Boys' dormitory.

munzi Ngoni village; group of hamlets.

Ngoma One-time Ngoni military dance that is now performed for entertainment.

nshlanze Wife who bears children for the king.

pfuko Ngoni clan; group of villages.

Umkulumqango The Great Spirit; supreme god of the Ngoni traditional religion.

For Further Reading

Crosby, Cynthia A. *Historical Dictionary of Malawi*, 2nd ed. London: Scarecrow Press, 1993.

O'Toole, Thomas. *Malawi in Pictures*. Minneapolis: Lerner, 1988.

Pachai, Bridglal, ed. *The Early History of Malawi*. London: Longman, 1972.

Phiri, D. D. *From Nguni to Ngoni*. Malawi: Popular Publications, 1982.

CHALLENGING READING

Read, Margaret. *The Ngoni of Nyasaland*. London: Frank Cass, 1970.

Index

A

amadlozi (ancestral spirits), 13, 42–44, 46, 48

B

beadwork, 36, 39–40
beer, 36, 43–44, 51
boys' dormitory (*laweni*), 32–34
bride-price, 12, 50, 52
burial, 45–49

C

captives, 26, 32, 38–40
cattle, 12–13, 41, 43, 48, 49, 52, 57, 58–59
Central Africa, 9, 20
chiefdoms, 9–16, 18
chiefs, 12–16, 29–30
Christianity, 48, 60
colonization, 10, 41, 54, 55–60

D

dance, 17
diviner, 43
divorce, 52

F

farming, 12, 54

G

gogo (grandmother; nurse), 32, 34–36
Gomani kingdom, 10
Great Wife, 22

H

hamlet, 31
herd boys, 32
hut tax, 55–56

I

impis (troops), 37, 56
inheritance, 53–54
inkosi (chief), 14, 29–30, 32, 38, 48–49, 54, 57, 58
izinduna (elders), 30, 32, 34, 41, 51, 54, 57

J

Jere Ngoni, 30, 32, 39, 40, 48, 52–53
history of, 10–12, 14, 18–26

K

kingdoms, 9–16

L

language, 10

M

mafuko (clan system), 31–32, 44
Malawi, region of, 10–12, 17, 19, 21, 24–27, 55, 56, 59, 60
marriage, 17, 38, 39, 49–53
Maseko Ngoni, 30, 32, 39–40, 48, 55–57
history of, 10–12, 14, 18–19, 21, 24, 26–27
Mfecane (migrations), 9–10,

18, 29, 30, 31–32, 37
military, 29, 32, 36–40
M'Mbelwa Jere, 10, 26, 55, 58–60
Mozambique, 10, 21, 24, 27, 56, 60
Mthethwa, 12, 14
music, 17

N
Ndwandwe, 12, 13, 15, 16
Nguni, 9, 12–16, 18, 36, 38
   customs, 13, 22, 29, 37–38, 60
Ngwane chiefdom, 12
North Nguni, 12

P
pottery, 36

R
religion, 13, 42–45, 59

S
Shaka, Chief, 14–16, 18–19,

36–38, 39
snuff, 43–45, 52–53
South Africa, 9, 12
spears, ancestral, 48

T
Tanzania, 10, 21, 24, 60
trade, 12, 13

V
villages, 31, 41, 51

W
warriors, 10, 17, 32, 33, 34, 37–38, 49–50, 57
witchcraft, 23

Z
Zambia, 10, 26, 60
Zulu, 12, 14–16
Zwangendaba, Chief, 14, 19–26, 30
Zwide, Chief, 13–16, 18, 30

ABOUT THE AUTHOR
Nwankwo Tony Nwaezeigwe holds both Bachelor and Master of Arts degrees in history from the University of Nigeria, Nsukka, where he currently lectures on African and Middle Eastern history. He has a special research interest in precolonial Igbo politics. His work has been widely published in scholarly journals.

ACKNOWLEDGMENTS
The publisher would like to thank Michael W. Conner, Ph.D., an expert on the Ngoni of Malawi, for his assistance with this volume.

PHOTO CREDITS: All photographs by Michael W. Conner, Ph.D.

CONSULTING EDITOR: Gary N. van Wyk, Ph.D.

LAYOUT AND DESIGN: Kim Sonsky